insight text guide

Maude Ashton

The Kite Runner

Khaled Hosseini

AF583722

insight®
innovative engaging evolving

Copyright © Insight Publications 2005

First published in 2005, reprinted 2006, 2007, 2008, 2009, 2012, 2015, 2016, 2017, 2018, 2019, 2020, 2021.

Insight Publications Pty Ltd
3/350 Charman Road
Cheltenham VIC 3192
Australia
Tel: +61 3 8571 4950
Fax: +61 3 8571 0257
Email: books@insightpublications.com.au

www.insightpublications.com.au

Copying for educational purposes

The Australian *Copyright Act 1968* (the Act) allows a maximum of one chapter or 10% of this book, whichever is the greater, to be copied by any educational institution for its educational purposes provided that the educational institution (or the body that administers it) has given a remuneration notice to Copyright Agency under the Act.

For details of the Copyright Agency licence for educational institutions contact:

Copyright Agency
Tel: +61 2 9394 7600
Fax: +61 2 9394 7601
www.copyright.com.au

Copying for other purposes

Except as permitted under the Act (for example, any fair dealing for the purposes of study, research, criticism or review) no part of this book may be reproduced, stored in a retrieval system, or transmitted in any form or by any means without prior written permission. All inquiries should be made to the publisher at the address above.

National Library of Australia Cataloguing-in-Publication entry:

Ashton, Maude.
Khaled Hosseini's The Kite runner : text guide.
For VCE English students.
ISBN 9781921088070
1. Hosseini, Khaled. The Kite runner. I. Title.
813.6

Cover design: The Modern Art Production Group

Printed in Australia by Ligare

contents

CHARACTER MAP

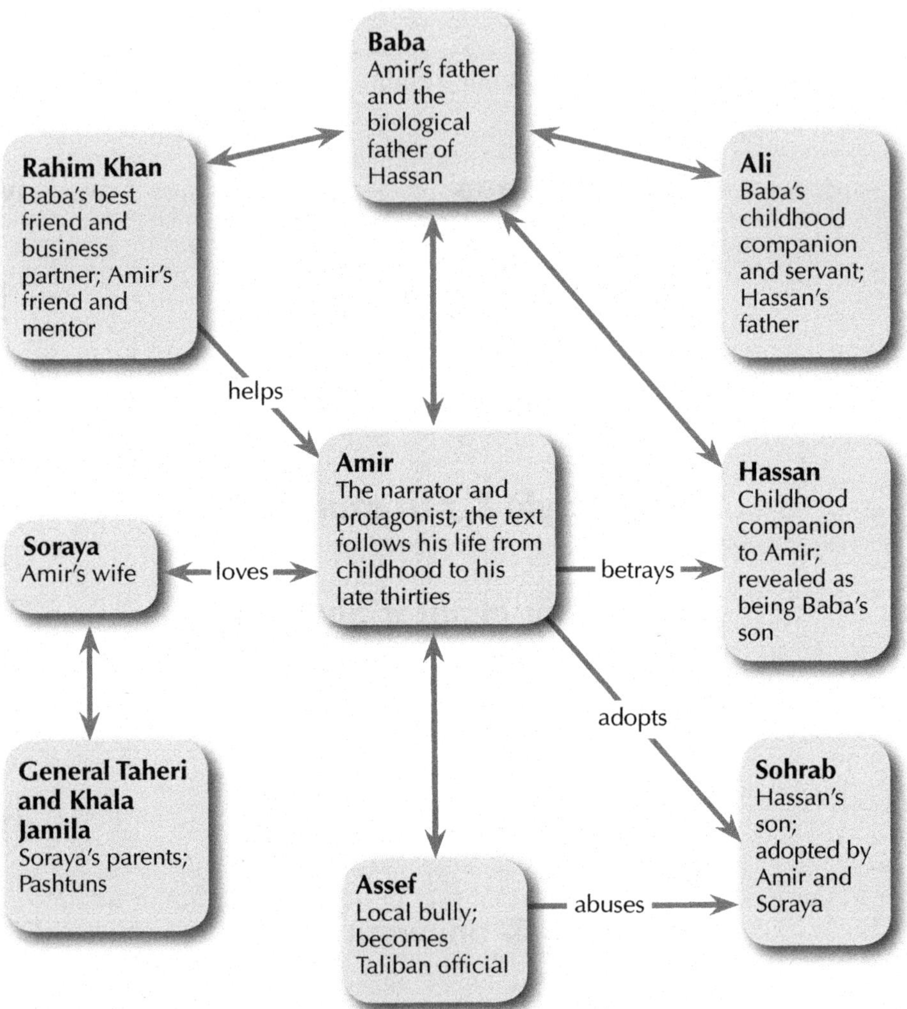

INTRODUCTION

The Kite Runner, Khaled Hosseini's first novel, has been a runaway bestseller, attracting huge readerships in America and throughout the world. Hosseini is an Afghan-American medical doctor who lives in California, having migrated to the United States as a refugee during the Soviet occupation of Afghanistan. The publishers of *The Kite Runner* tell us that this is the first novel written in English by an Afghan.

Hosseini was born in Afghanistan in 1965, the oldest of five children. His mother was a teacher of Farsi and history in Kabul and his father was a diplomat. When Hosseini was eleven, his father moved with his family to Paris as part of his work commitments. In 1980, while Afghanistan was occupied by the Soviet Union, the family sought political asylum in the US. Hosseini moved with his family to San Jose, California, in 1980.

Autobiographical aspects of *The Kite Runner*

There are some clear parallels between Hosseini's own life and that of the protagonist of *The Kite Runner,* Amir. Hosseini had a privileged life in Kabul which was much like the life Amir leads. The text evokes the sense of place very clearly and richly, both in the early chapters in Kabul and in the flea market in San Jose. Hosseini has acknowledged that the setting for the early part of the novel, with its descriptions of the house Amir grows up in and even the name of the suburb that Amir lives in, Wazir Akbar Khan, is 'almost directly lifted from my own life'.[1] Hosseini has also indicated that his description of the Afghan section of the San Jose flea market is based on his own experience of it.

As well as the setting of the text in both Afghanistan and America, the larger political background which is woven through the novel is taken from life. Although *The Kite Runner* was written before Hosseini returned to Afghanistan, he had been part of the Afghan-American community who relayed to each other the details of life in Afghanistan throughout its tumultuous recent political history.

---

1 Khaled Hosseini in an interview with Kerri Miller, 'Author is inspired by memories of Afghanistan', Minnesota Public Radio, 5 May 2004, http://news.minnesota.publicradio.org/programs/midmorning/listings/mm20040503.shtml

BACKGROUND & CONTEXT

Political background

Afghanistan became the focus of world attention in the last two decades of the twentieth century, most notably because of the Soviet invasion of Afghanistan and the Taliban's activities. Khaled Hosseini's novel is set mainly in Kabul, Afghanistan's capital, during the markedly contrasting periods of Afghanistan's modern history: the rule of the monarchy and that of the Taliban. In order to gain a deeper understanding of the text you will need to know something of Afghanistan's twentieth century political history.

The relative peace that marked the reign of the king, Zahir Shah, from 1933 to 1973 provides the background for the chapters dealing with Amir's childhood in Kabul. However, Afghanistan became unstable in the 1970s when the Communist Party and the Islamic movement became antagonists in a battle for power over the country.

In 1979 the Soviet Union (the USSR) invaded Afghanistan to prevent the Islamic militia (later known as the Mujahedin, or 'holy warriors') from taking power. The USSR wanted to keep Afghanistan under its influence so the US, a traditional enemy of the USSR, provided support and weapons to the Mujahedin to help them remove the Soviet army from Afghanistan. It was during this time of Soviet rule that Amir and Baba fled Afghanistan to take refuge in the United States. The Soviet troops remained in Afghanistan until 1989.

The 1990s saw the Mujahedin come to power. However, ethnic factions in the Mujahedin continued to contest the leadership of the country, leading to four years of civil war from 1992 to 1996. The constant state of turmoil in the country caused by the clash among the ethnic groups in the Mujahedin created support amongst Afghans for the Taliban.

The Taliban, which was established on fundamentalist Islamic principles, was formed by Afghan Islamic clerics and students, and one of its major aims was to enforce strict conformity with Islamic customs. Once it gained political control of Afghanistan in 1996–1997, the Taliban established the Ministry for the Promotion of Virtue and the Suppression of Vice to police compliance with the tenets of Islam. In *The Kite Runner*, it is during the period of the Taliban's rule that Amir returns to Kabul, where he witnesses the Taliban's constant surveillance of the Afghan people and the public stoning to death of a man and woman accused of adultery.

After the 11 September terrorist attacks in 2001, the US and the UK launched air strikes against Afghanistan which led to the fall of the Taliban government in November 2001. In 2004 Afghanistan elected Hamid Karzai as president.

Religion

Religion plays an important part in *The Kite Runner*, either as an set of beliefs open to dispute, as it is for Baba, or as a source of immutable truths which are taken as the central tenets for government, as in the case of the Taliban. At the beginning of the text Amir is undecided about religion: 'Caught between Baba and the mullahs at school, I still hadn't made up my mind about God' (p.55). However, he becomes a devout Muslim by the end of the text.

While Afghanistan is largely a mosaic of languages and ethnicities, the uniting factor in the country is that ninety-nine per cent of the population is Muslim. However, within the overarching Muslim religion there are two main Muslim sects in Afghanistan. Eighty per cent of the Muslim population is Sunni Muslim, and the remaining twenty per cent is Shi'a. Membership of each sect is linked to ethnicity so, for example, most ethnic Hazaras are also Shi'a Muslims. Amir, Baba and their immediate circle are Sunni Muslims, while Ali and Hassan are Shi'a Muslims. The distinction between Shi'a and Sunni sects is as important as the distinction between Pashtun and Hazara ethnic groups, and it is also a source of discrimination against Hassan and Ali.

The Kite Runner is critical of the discrimination against Shi'a Muslims by the majority Sunni Muslims in Afghanistan. The book also argues against the fundamentalist Muslim practices of the Taliban, but this should not be read as an anti-Muslim stance. In fact, the critique that Amir offers of the Taliban and its practices is that they do not honour the spirit of Islam. For instance, when Assef, the Taliban official, tells Amir he is on a mission from God, Amir lists the atrocities the Taliban has committed and demands to know how Assef could justify these "in the name of Islam" (p.248).

Ethnic groups

The central characters in *The Kite Runner* come from different ethnic groups and it is important to understand the emphasis that Hosseini gives to ethnicity and its effect on people's lives. Also there are many different ethnic groups in Afghanistan, it is only the main groups which are referred to in the text that are discussed below.

Pashtun

This is the largest and traditionally the ruling ethnic group in Afghanistan; Amir and Baba are Pashtuns. Most Pashtuns are Sunni Muslims. The following description of Pashtun (also known as Pushtun) culture is particularly helpful in understanding Baba's personality and his opposition to parts of Islamic law (known as Shariah):

> Pushtun culture rests on *Pushtunwali,* a legal and moral code that determines social order and responsibilities. It contains sets of values pertaining to honor (*namuz*), solidarity (*nang*), hospitality, mutual support, shame and revenge which determines social order and individual responsibility. The defense of *namuz*, even unto death, is obligatory for every Pushtun. Elements in this code of behavior are often in opposition to the Shariah. Much of the resistance to the largely detribalized leadership of the DRA stemmed from the perception that in attempting to nationalize land and wealth, as well as regulate marriage practices, the DRA was unlawfully violating the prescriptions of *Pushtunwali.*[2]

(Note: DRA is an acronym for the Democratic Republic of Afghanistan, 1978–1992, when it was ruled by a pro-Soviet government.)

2 AllRefer.com – Afghanistan, http://reference.allrefer.com/country-guide-study/afghanistan.html (website no longer available)

Hazara

Ali and Hassan are ethnically Hazaras and in terms of their religion Shi'a Muslims. Hazaras have suffered a great deal of persecution, especially under the Taliban. Hazaras are traditionally agrarian people, many of whom have been forced to seek work in the cities. They were often servants to the wealthy in Kabul.

Other ethnic groups

The Kite Runner also mentions the ethnicity of Amir's driver, Farid, who is a Tajik. Tajiks comprise the second-largest ethnic group in Afghanistan. Other ethnic groups in Afghanistan include the Kyrgyz, Turkmen, Baluchi, Uzbek, Nuristani and Ismaili groups. These groups do not feature in the text but it is important to realise that Afghanistan's population is not homogeneous. This fact has contributed greatly both to the political unrest in Afghanistan. Furthermore, your membership of a particular ethnic group has an enormous influence on the position you occupy in the social hierarchy.

Amir and Hassan's ethnic differences

Amir, as a Pashtun, is separated from Hassan not only by class and religious differences but also, despite their both being Afghans, by the enormous chasm of their ethnicity. You will notice that throughout the text the relationship between Amir and Hassan is frequently scrutinised by disapproving onlookers. Indeed, the value of Hassan's very existence is often questioned by other characters in the text. It would be useful to make a table noting each reference to Hassan as a Hazara, including what people say about him and their attitude to the Hazara people.

Qaom

Qaom (also spelled *qaum*) is a unit of Afghan society that links individuals to a larger group. You may find that Baba's parties and excursions involve a bewildering variety of people; you might also notice that many different people who seem to have nothing in common visit Baba when he is in hospital. The Afghan notion of *Qaom* helps to explain this.

Qaom works most strongly within the family, then the tribe, clan, ethnic group and region. *Qaom* is contextual; that is, when two Afghans from the same mountain area belong to different tribes they may show animosity to one another, but when the same two individuals meet in Kabul or in America they are part of the same *qaom* because they come from the same area. *Qaom* works to support the individuals within it, giving them aid when they need it and providing protection from outsiders. *Qaom* is as important as ethnic background as a marker of identity.

Cultural context

One of the highlights of this text is the insight that the reader is given into Afghan families, relationships, celebrations, customs and rituals. We learn some things about Afghan culture because the narrator gives us the information directly, such as: 'Afghans are an independent people. Afghans cherish custom but abhor rules' (p.45). However, much of the spirit of Afghan culture comes to us through Hosseini's description of gatherings of families, friends and *qaom*.

While war and political turmoil in Afghanistan have been the focus of international concern in the last three decades, Hosseini's text draws attention to the life that goes on beyond the focus of the media's cameras. Both in Afghanistan and in America, he says, the way of life of his compatriots continues with all its virtues, such as hospitality and loyalty, and its flaws, as instanced in the gossip and discrimination that happens on a daily basis.

A short Afghan vocabulary

Afghan – someone from Afghanistan. An Afghani is a unit of money in Afghanistan.

Iftikhar – pride.

Mujahedin – literally means 'struggler': one who engages in a jihad or struggle. The Mujahedin ruled Afghanistan from 1992 to 1996.

Namoos – pride.

Nazr – sacrificing an animal (in *The Kite Runner* this is usually a sheep) as part of a religious vow.

Parchami – Afghan Communist Party.

Shorawi – occupying Soviet forces in Afghanistan.

Taliban – 'Talib' literally means 'student'. Taliban is the name of the Islamic fundamentalist political party which was in power from 1996 to 2001.

Zakat – giving money to the needy.

GENRE, STRUCTURE & STYLE

Genre: the *bildungsroman*

Khaled Hosseini is credited with having written the first novel in English by an Afghan writer. *The Kite Runner* belongs to a familiar genre, known as the *bildungsroman*, which explores the development from childhood to adulthood of a character who usually undergoes some form of crisis which shapes their personality. There are many examples in literature of this genre and you might like to look at some of the more famous ones in order to get a sense of the characteristics of the genre. Some examples of a type of this genre where the character eventually becomes an artist like Amir, who becomes a writer, include *A Portrait of the Artist as a Young Man* by James Joyce and *The Man Who Loved Children* by Christina Stead.

A three-part structure

The structure of *The Kite Runner* can be usefully seen as working in three parts. Hosseini divides the text into three sections that correspond with important parts of Amir's life. The first part follows Amir's childhood in Afghanistan. The second part depicts his adulthood in America and the final section traces his return to Afghanistan and the events following that trip. The very short opening chapter links the three sections in this broader structure and serves to introduce us to Amir's quest.

The text begins at crucial point in Amir's life, with a telephone call that will call him back to the country of his childhood, where he will revisit his homeland and confront his past mistakes. This structure allows Hosseini to do two important things. Firstly, in the context of the characters and plot, he prepares the reader for a crisis that disturbs what would seem to be an almost idyllic childhood, were it not for the unexplained withholding of love by Baba. Secondly, on a broader scale, the structure forces two cultures, those of Afghanistan and America, into juxtaposition. This means that the reader is invited to make comparisons between the values inherent in those very different cultures.

Language: the image of the lamb

A strong metaphor which Hosseini uses throughout the novel is that of the sacrificial lamb. This image occurs several times in *The Kite Runner* and it has a number of connotations. A lamb denotes innocence and purity, but it can also call to mind the image of a 'sacrificial lamb', a lamb that is offered up to appease an angry deity or as part of a religious ceremony when making asking God for a favour.

The image of a lamb can be traced through the novel, particularly in relation to Hassan and Sohrab. Both characters are innocents and both have been sacrificed in some way. A shocking image of Hassan as a sacrificial lamb is used in the rape scene. When Amir witnesses the rape of Hassan he describes 'the resignation' in Hassan's face as 'a look I had seen before ... the look of the lamb' (p.66). Amir is referring to the sacrificial lamb that is offered as part of a *nazr* ceremony to obtain help from God, but the image is a brutal one since Hassan is absolutely powerless in this situation and the image seems to imply that Hassan is resigned to being sacrificed for Amir's sake. When Amir witnesses the real sacrifice of a lamb each year in his own backyard he feels there is a 'look of acceptance in the animal's eyes', and he tells the reader: 'I imagine the animal understands. I imagine the animal sees that its imminent demise is for a higher purpose. This is the look ...' (p.67). Amir leaves this sentence unfinished. In juxtaposing this scene with that of Hassan's rape, he implies that Hassan accepts the assault against him. This is further confirmed by the passage that follows:

> Maybe Hassan was the price I had to pay, the lamb I had to slay, to win Baba. Was it a fair price? The answer floated to my conscious mind before I could thwart it: He was just a Hazara, wasn't he? (p.68)

Sohrab, too, is described as having 'slaughter sheep's eyes' (p.249), but Amir has matured enough to understand that no-one is of such a lowly status that they can be offered as a sacrifice for a perceived 'higher purpose', and he is able to interpret Sohrab's look correctly as pleading with him to save him.

Tone

Since Amir is the narrator, much of the tone of the text is attributable to his personal characteristics. For the most part, Amir narrates the events of the text and his own thoughts and feelings in a reflective and self-deprecating tone. He is quick to attribute his failings to flaws in his own character rather than ascribing them to the circumstances in which he lives.

Amir's narration varies in tone, however, depending on the scene he is describing. There is a lyrical tone used in the early chapters in his description of his childhood in Kabul:

> Sometimes my entire childhood seems like one long lazy summer day with Hassan, chasing each other between tangles of trees in my father's yard, playing hide-and-seek, cops and robbers, cowboys and Indians ... (p.22)

At other times, monumental, history-changing statements are made in a portentous tone. A good example of this kind of statement introduces the fall of the monarchy: '"Well," I began. But I never got to finish that sentence. Because suddenly Afghanistan changed forever.' (p.30)

These momentous statements, which are used quite liberally throughout the text, are appropriate to the dramatic themes and ideas with which *The Kite Runner* deals. The war in Afghanistan and the major upheavals in personal relationships, such as Amir's betrayal of Hassan, lead to these declamatory statements, but these passages contrast sharply with the overall tone of the text which is written in an informal, conversational style.

Style

Hosseini intended to write a novel about Afghanistan which showed its readers that there was more to that country than the wars, the Taliban's activities and the links with terrorism which had characterised it in the media. He wanted to show that there had been a peaceful, harmonious time in Afghanistan which had preceded the tumultuous events of the late twentieth century. In an interview with the *San Francisco Chronicle* Hosseini says:

> Too often stories about Afghanistan center around the various wars, the opium trade, the war on terrorism. Precious little is said about the Afghan people themselves – their culture, their traditions, how they lived in their country and how they manage abroad as exiles.[3]

In keeping with the aims of the novel, much of the writing has an implied American audience. Hosseini takes great pains to explain in English the Afghan words used throughout the novel, and he provides the reader with the historical and cultural background to Afghanistan that would be unknown to most English-speaking readers.

Hosseini's writing style is, on the whole, casual and conversational, making the novel very accessible. He uses a number of colloquialisms, such as Amir's reply of "Whatever" (p.51) to Hassan's declaration that he likes his home. Hosseini also uses the unfinished sentence structures that are characteristic of speech patterns, such as: 'Someplace with no ghosts, no memories, and no sins' (p.119), 'Which was ironic' (p.41), and 'Back to my old life' (p.58).

Hosseini is also influenced, to some degree, by the style of fables in the writing of this text. The characters in the text have qualities which make them larger than life: they are often readily identifiable with archetypes in literature. The characters of Baba and Assef are very strongly written in the style of the heroic father and the evil villain. Sohrab is named after a famous son in the fable of Rostam and Sohrab, which is the children's favourite story (p.25). Hassan, in his innocence and nobility of spirit, represents goodness: he is also 'the face of Afghanistan' and, in many ways, his fate runs parallel with the fate of Afghanistan.

Deriving from the fable genre, too, is Hosseini's use of repetition and parallels in working out the morality of the narrative. Amir is faced with the same situation as an adult that he baulked at as a child. However, as

---

3 Khaled Hosseini, cited by Edward Guthmann in the *San Francisco Chronicle*, 14 March 2005, http://www.sfgate.com/cgi-bin/article.cgi?f=/c/a/2005/03/14/DDGNDBOF471.DTL

an adult who has learned an important lesson he is able to save Sohrab from Assef. Hassan and Amir grow up as 'two halves' (p.313) who do not know their true relationship with one another, and Amir dreams of Assef as his malevolent 'twin' (p.268). Another singular parallel is that Amir, in seeking redemption for his sins against Hassan, acquires the same scar as Hassan when his lip is split in the centre by Assef.

Narrative point of view

Amir is the narrator of *The Kite Runner*. He narrates the events of the novel retrospectively, as an adult looking back on the past. Since Amir is both a character in the novel and the narrator, he can tell the story only from his own point of view, and he therefore does not have access to 'the truth' as he cannot possibly know what other characters are thinking and feeling. Similarly, Amir cannot know what has happened before his lifetime, unless another character relates that information to him, nor can he know what will happen in the future (in the way that an omniscient narrator can).

For a further discussion of Amir's role as narrator, see 'Amir as narrator' in the characters & relationships section.

One chapter – chapter sixteen – is narrated by Rahim Khan, Amir's trusted friend and mentor, who recounts the events that occurred in Afghanistan while Baba and Amir were living in America. By using this new narrator, Hosseini allows Amir to gain further insight into Baba's character. This insight comes from knowledge that only Rahim Khan has. Hosseini builds up dramatic tension by maintaining Amir's limited point of view to guide the reader's interpretation of events. The subsequent introduction of Rahim Khan's voice allows us to understand some of the ambiguities that Amir felt were present in his relationship with his father.

CHAPTER-BY-CHAPTER ANALYSIS

One (pp.1–2)

Summary: *Set in December 2001, the protagonist remembers two events: one, an incident in a deserted alley in 1975; the other, a phone call during the last summer from his friend, Rahim Khan, asking him to go to Pakistan.*

In this brief opening chapter we learn that the as yet unnamed protagonist has been haunted by an event in his childhood for the past twenty-six years. The chapter is set in San Francisco, but we know that this is probably not the location of the childhood memories since the names of the other characters mentioned, Hassan, Ali and Baba, seem to be associated with Kabul, the capital of Afghanistan.

In this chapter the narrator mentions the main characters in the text and indicates the central issue around which the text is built – that is, a 'past of unatoned sins' (p.1) which follows a life-changing event. The narrator also alerts us to the possibility of atonement in Rahim Khan's last words on the telephone: *'There is a way to be good again'* (p.2).

Q What are your first impressions of Amir in this chapter?

Two (pp.3–10)

Summary: *As children, Hassan and Amir are playing in the garden of the house belonging to Baba, Amir's father. The house is in a wealthy suburb of Kabul; Hassan and his father, Ali, live in a mud hut at the end of the garden. Hassan is taunted by soldiers and Ali by the older children in the neighbourhood.*

The second chapter is set in the more distant past of Amir's childhood. Amir is the protagonist and the narrator, and the reader sees the events of his childhood from Amir's point of view, as an adult who is looking back on his childhood.

Amir is the more powerful of the two boys, persuading Hassan to shine mirrors in the neighbours' windows and pelting a neighbour's dog with walnuts. Hassan possesses a quieter power, however, protecting Amir from blame for the actions that he initiates and shouldering responsibility for their actions when Ali confronts the boys.

One of the reminders of Amir's mother is her library, which is still intact in Baba's study, and it is through reading one of his mother's books that Amir begins to understand something of the prejudice that surrounds Ali and Hassan: it is because they are ethnic Hazaras.

Q Compare Amir's attitude to Hazaras with that of his teacher.

Three (pp.11-20)

Summary: *Baba's character: he is compared to a bear and a hurricane; he sees things in black and white; Baba builds an orphanage and dismisses religious fundamentalism; he is disappointed in Amir.*

In this chapter Baba's character is developed in more detail. Since Amir is the narrator, a great deal of what he tells us is from his perspective as the child of a very powerful man. For this reason, Baba appears to be like a character from a fable who fights bears with his bare hands, whose snores echo through the house and whose judgments are unshakable.

Amir's difficult relationship with Baba is constantly mediated by Rahim Khan, who defends Amir's sensitivity as the lack of "a mean streak" (p.20). Amir, is sceptical of this assessment of his characters, saying he 'had been wrong about the mean streak thing' (p.20). The narrator refers to his treatment of Hassan on the following morning, implicitly reminding the reader of the incident in the alley alluded to in the first chapter.

Q Is Rahim Khan correct in saying that Amir lacks a 'mean streak'?

Four (pp.21-30)

Summary: *Ali and Baba grow up as playmates, just as Amir and Hassan do; Amir reads Hassan stories; Hassan and Rahim Khan appreciate the stories that Amir writes but Baba dismisses his writing.*

As the chapter opens the narrative moves back to 1933, the year that Baba was born and Ali was adopted into Baba's father's household. The narrator juxtaposes the childhoods of Ali and Baba as playmates with that of Amir and Hassan. In many ways their experiences are very similar, since the relationships between the playmates never quite become full friendships. Ethnic, religious and class barriers prevent the existence of such a friendship in Afghan culture since, as Amir explains:

> history isn't easy to overcome. Neither is religion. In the end, I was a Pashtun and he was a Hazara, I was Sunni and he was Shi'a, and nothing was ever going to change that. Nothing. (p.22)

Many of the scenes from Hassan and Amir's childhood seem idyllic, and the heightened, poetic style of the writing reflects the narrator's idealised memories of his friendship with Hassan. For instance, he recalls Hassan '[s]itting cross-legged, sunlight and shadows of pomegranate leaves dancing on his face ... as I read him stories he couldn't read for himself' (p.24). This tranquillity is soon undercut, however, by Amir's small acts of cruelty to Hassan, such as giving Hassan the incorrect meaning of the word 'imbecile' and applying it to Hassan (p.25). Amir cannot rid himself of a nagging feeling of guilt about the way he treats Hassan.

Amir, too, is subject to casual cruelty from his father, whose lack of interest in his son's writing provokes a dramatic outburst of anger: 'right then, I wished I could open my veins and drain his cursed blood from my body' (p.27). Once again, Baba's dismissive reaction to Amir is contrasted with the congratulations Amir elicits from Rahim Khan and Hassan.

Q Do you think that Baba is an uncaring and distant father? Why?

Five (pp.31–41)

Summary: *Gunfire and explosions in Kabul frighten Hassan and Amir; the bully, Assef, threatens Hassan and Amir, but Hassan stands up to him; Baba pays for the surgical repair of Hassan cleft palate as a birthday gift to him.*

On 17 July 1973 the monarchy is overthrown and Amir and Hassan witness the night of the coup. The change in Afghanistan's political history also marks a change in the lives of Hassan and Amir, since this is when they earn the enmity of Assef, the savage local bully. It is no coincidence that Assef, the most evil character in the text, strongly supports the fall of the monarchy and admires Hitler.

Assef enunciates the belief about the Hazaras that has up till now been in the background of the story. This is that Afghanistan belongs to the Pashtuns, who are 'the pure Afghans' (p.35). The issue of ethnic divisions rises to prominence again and again throughout the text, and Hosseini presents the reader, through his portrayal of the relationship of Amir and Hassan, with the significance of these divisions within Afghanistan.

Amir's confusion over his father's love for Hassan and Baba's apparent rejection of Amir increases when Dr Kumar, the surgeon, appears as Hassan's 'present'. Amir's jealousy of Hassan arises once more since 'Hassan hadn't done anything to earn Baba's affections' (p.40).

Q Assef says that Hazaras 'pollute our homeland'? What does Hosseini achieve by having Assef assert this prejudice?

Six (pp.42–51)

Summary: *Winter in Kabul is the season for the kite-fighting tournament; Amir feels closer to Baba because of his kite-fighting ability; in the winter of 1975, Amir decides to win the competition and thereby win his father's approval.*

Once again in recounting the memories of Amir and Hassan's childhood the writing becomes lyrical: winter is a time of 'playing cards by the stove with Hassan, free Russian movies on Tuesday mornings at Cinema Park, sweet turnip *qurma* over rice for lunch after a morning of building snowmen' (p.42). For Amir, however, the kite-flying tournament has greater significance than a game. Amir thinks that by winning the competition he will also win Baba's approval, thereby showing his father 'once and for all that his son was worthy'. Then, Amir concludes, his 'life as a ghost in this house would finally be over' (p.49).

Amir's assumption that Baba's approval would follow a demonstration of his prowess in kite fighting is fuelled by his feeling that his father blames him for his mother's death in childbirth. There is a desperation behind Amir's determination to win and this, coupled with Hassan's willingness to let Amir win even their card games, creates a sense of foreboding in the reader.

Q Why is Amir so desperate to win his father's approval?

Seven (pp.52–69)

Summary: *Hassan dreams that Amir conquers the monster in the lake; Amir automatically prays to win the competition; Amir wins the competition and Hassan, the kite runner, races to retrieve the losing kite; Assef and his followers trap Hassan in an alley and Assef rapes Hassan; Amir sees the rape but runs away, pretending that nothing has happened; Amir accepts his father's congratulations.*

Key scene

Amir witnesses the rape of his childhood companion, Hassan, but does nothing to protect him. This is the central event in the text and the event that has haunted Amir all his life. Amir's cowardice seems inexplicable and the reader feels some repulsion at Amir's failure to defend his playmate, but that disgust is also shared by Amir himself. Amir feels that his abandonment of his friend is worse than cowardice: he sees it as sacrificing Hassan in order to win Baba's approval. Amir fears that he allows Hassan to be raped since he is 'just a Hazara' (p.68). The image of the slaughtered lamb (see the section on 'Language' for further discussion of this image) which recurs throughout the text and is developed further in this scene reinforces the idea that Amir gives Hassan up in order to win his father's approval.

Earlier in the chapter, Hassan recalls his dream to Amir and in doing so reveals that he is not only a very considerate friend, but is also very tactful in dispelling Amir's fears (pp.52–3).

After winning the contest, Amir searches for Hassan. He encounters Omar , a merchant in the bazaar who is 'a pretty good guy' (p.60), then Hassan's attackers, Assef, Wali and Kamal (p.62). Each of these characters, either casually or with calculated violence, makes some attack on Hassan's ethnicity. Hosseini shows through these incidents how deeply embedded the idea of the inferiority of the Hazaras is.

Q What is your opinion of Amir's actions in this chapter?

Q What does the image of the lamb contribute to your understanding of Amir and Hassan?

Eight (pp.70–87)

Summary: *Hassan retreats to his room to recover; Baba, Amir and a large group of family and friends make a trip to Jalalabad; Hassan and Amir drift further apart; Amir's thirteenth birthday party.*

The relationship between Amir and Baba improves following Amir's victory in the kite-fighting tournament, confirming Amir's supposition that Baba's approval is based on his son's being more like him. As this relationship improves, tension increases between Amir and Hassan, due to Amir's guilt at having deserted Hassan when he was being raped.

The trip to Jalalabad and Amir's birthday party provide more insights into daily life in Baba's *qaom*. What was planned as a small day out turns into an excursion of 'two dozen people' (p.72), travelling in three vans to Jalalabad. Amir sees the hundreds of guests at his birthday party and the mounting pile of presents as a tribute to the power of his father and examples of 'blood money' (p.89). Amir's enjoyment of his time with his father is partially spoilt by the inclusion of so many other people, but his real unhappiness stems from his betrayal of Hassan.

Amir goes out of his way to avoid Hassan, finally enraging his father by suggesting that he dismiss Ali and Hassan. In this way, Amir hopes to rid himself of the constant reminders of his mistreatment of Hassan.

Q Why does Amir describe his presents as 'blood money'? How does this affect your understanding of the father–son relationship?

Nine (pp.88–95)

Summary: *Amir hides his new watch and some of his birthday money under Hassan's mattress, then accuses Hassan of theft; Hassan admits to the theft he did not commit in order to protect Amir; Ali and Hassan leave the house despite Baba's protests.*

Amir receives two significant presents amongst the many he is given on his birthday. One is the writing journal Rahim Khan gives him in order to encourage his writing. The other is a beautiful copy of *Shahnamah*, the stories that Amir and Hassan love to read, given to him by Ali and Hassan: it is obviously an expensive gift that they can barely afford.

Amir executes his plan to have Ali and Hassan dismissed from Baba's household. Two surprising things happen as a result of Amir's incrimination of Hassan: Baba offers his forgiveness for the theft, and Ali is cold and unforgiving toward Amir. Amir's initial betrayal of Hassan is further compounded by his lies and efforts to dispossess Ali and Hassan of the only home they have known. Added to that, Amir causes his father enormous grief by separating him from his lifelong companion, Ali and, as we later learn, his illegitimate son, Hassan.

Q How does Hosseini maintain our sympathy for Amir in this chapter?

Ten: March 1981 (pp.96–108)

Summary: *Baba and Amir secretly leave Shorawi-occupied Afghanistan for Pakistan; a Russian soldier threatens to rape one of the Afghan refugees at the border and Baba intervenes; Baba and Amir hide with thirty other Afghans in a basement in Jalalabad; they are eventually transported to Pakistan in an empty petrol tanker.*

The narrative moves forward by five years to Amir and Baba's escape from Soviet-occupied Kabul. Baba is still a larger-than-life presence in Amir's eyes: when Baba confronts the Russian soldier 'he eclipsed the moonlight' (p.100). Amir's admiration for his father is tempered by the knowledge that such heroism might get them killed. Strangely, at the moment when a gun goes off and there is a possibility that Baba has been killed, Amir's first thoughts are about himself: 'I'm eighteen and alone. I have no one left in the world. Baba's dead and now I have to bury him' (p.101).

Amir continues to debate with himself the existence of God, at first praying automatically when he is under threat and later admiring his father's quick-witted response to the other refugees' admonitions to pray (p.104).

Kamal, one of Assef's gang of bullies, appears again in this chapter. Kamal has been raped and broken by this experience, and he eventually dies after the long trip in the petrol tanker.

Q Do you think that Amir is emotionally mature at this stage in his life? Give reasons for your answer and refer to events and dialogue in this chapter to support your point of view.

Eleven: Fremont, California, 1980s (pp.109–24)

Summary: *Baba and Amir emigrate and Baba has difficulty adjusting to America, but maintains his independent political views; Baba takes a job and refuses food stamps; Amir graduates from high school and enrols in junior college; Baba and Amir begin to work at the San Jose flea market with fellow Afghan refugees.*

Baba's furious outburst at the local grocery shop highlights the cultural differences that make his adjustment to America difficult. He interprets the Nguyens' request for identification in cashing a cheque as demonstrating a lack of trust in him and therefore an insult to his pride. Baba's values, which are entirely appropriate for a life in Afghanistan, are ill-suited to a life in America. His refusal of food stamps is also based on pride: one of his greatest fears is 'that an Afghan would see him buying food with charity money' (p.114).

In choosing a creative writing course instead of law or medicine, Amir angers his father but decides that he will persist in doing what he wants rather than give in to the guilt that he feels about his father's hard work. Amir justifies his decision by saying: 'The last time I had done that, I had damned myself' (p.117).

The flea market allows the Afghan population to create an improvised *qaom* of people who knew one another in Kabul. It is a source of 'Tea, Politics, and Scandal' (p.120) for the Afghan community, and it is at the flea market that Amir meets Soraya, the woman who will become his wife.

Q Does Amir blame his father for faults which are really his own?

Twelve (pp.125–44)

Summary: *Amir continues his guarded courtship of Soraya; Amir gives Soraya one of his short stories; her father, General Taheri, throws the story in the rubbish to protect his daughter from gossip; Baba has cancer and his death is imminent; Amir and Soraya become engaged.*

An important part of this chapter is set in the Afghan section of the flea market. It is here that Afghan immigrants to America have set up their own, smaller version of the society they left behind in their homeland. Many cultural identifiers are brought to the fore in this microcosm: General Taheri is 'a Pashtun to the root' (p.126), and Baba offers this description as a warning to Amir about approaching Soraya, the General's daughter. The protocol which surrounds the women in Pashtun society must be strictly followed in order to prevent disgracing Pashtun men.

Amir's vacillating belief in the existence of God comes into greater focus with the news of Baba's cancer. Since he knows Baba's attitude to religion he waits until he is asleep then prays for his father; still unsure, however, whether God exists.

Q What is the narrator's attitude to the double standards that apply to Afghan women and men?

Thirteen (pp.145-65)

Summary: *Amir and Soraya are betrothed and married; Baba dies; Soraya enrols in a teaching course; Amir's novel is accepted for publication; the USSR withdraws from Afghanistan; Soraya and Amir discuss adopting a child.*

General Taheri's house contains many of the same cultural indicators as that of Baba in Kabul, including a photograph of Zahir Shah, the deposed King of Afghanistan. These indicate the families' culture and social status. Much of this chapter allows the reader to understand some of the customs and culture surrounding Afghan ceremonies. Hosseini explains the significance of moments in the wedding and funeral ceremonies that Amir is involved in.

The introduction of Soraya's character into the text allows for more discussion of the role of women in Afghan society. She highlights the double standard applied to men and women in that society.

Amir reflects that during his whole life he has been 'Baba's son' (p.152), and that his status in the world will change with Baba's death. However, Amir's guilt about Hassan surfaces again when he finds that he and Soraya cannot have children and he suggests that 'perhaps something, someone, somewhere, had decided to deny me fatherhood for the things I had done' (p.164).

Q Amir mourns the death of his father, but can you think of any ways in which Baba's death is a release for Amir?

Fourteen (pp.166-9)

Summary: *Rahim Khan telephones from Pakistan to ask Amir to return there; Amir realises that Rahim Khan knows about what happened to Hassan.*

The narrative now links with the opening chapter by referring to the phone call from Rahim Khan. Amir's decision to go to Pakistan is an important one, since he feels that it is a chance to achieve salvation or, as Rahim Khan says, 'a way to be good again' (p.168).

Q How successful is this chapter as a linking device between the past and the time in which it is set?

Fifteen (pp.170-7)

Summary: *Amir arrives in Pakistan; Rahim Khan tells him about the brutality of the Taliban; Amir learns that Rahim Khan will soon die.*

Amir learns about conditions in Kabul where, as Rahim Khan tells him, the Northern Alliance "did more damage ... than the Shorawi" (p.174), and the Taliban have since ruled with violence and thuggery. Rahim Khan praises America's optimism and tells Amir, "[t]here is such a thing as God's will" (p.176). Rahim Khan has been an influential person in Amir's development but Amir counters his statement about God by echoing his father's sentiments: "There is only what you do and what you don't do" (p.176).

Q What is Rahim Khan's attitude to America? How does it compare to Baba's opinion of America?

Sixteen (pp.178-87)

Summary: *Rahim Khan travels to Hazarajat to find Hassan; Hassan is married to Farzana; Rahim Khan persuades them to return with him to Kabul; Farzana's first baby is stillborn, then Farzana and Hassan have a son, Sohrab; Hassan's mother, Sanaubar, returns; in 1996, the Taliban take over government.*

Key point

Rahim Khan narrates this chapter, which covers the events in Kabul since Amir's departure. Since so much time has elapsed, the narrative moves forward with some speed, covering many events, both domestic and political. There is also a change in tone in this chapter, as it is related by Rahim Khan; the tone here is more philosophical, accepting events as they happen. Rahim Khan uses phrases such as "Allah forgive me" (p.184) and 'Allah was kind to us' (p.186). There is affection, untinged by guilt, in Rahim Khan's description of Hassan.

The political changes that have affected Kabul are greeted differently by Rahim Khan and Hassan. While Rahim Khan was initially happy about the political takeover by the Taliban, Hassan greets this news with 'a sober look in his eyes' (p.186). Hassan's fears are confirmed when we learn that in 1998 the Taliban massacred the Hazaras in Mazar-i-Sharif (p.187).

Q Rahim Khan is the only other character to narrate a part of the story. What perspective does he add to the telling of the story?

Seventeen (pp.188–95)

Summary: *Rahim Khan gives Amir letters from Hassan; he tells Amir that Hassan and his wife have been executed by the Taliban; Rahim Khan asks Amir to rescue Hassan's son from Kabul and reveals that Hassan was the illegitimate son of Baba and, therefore, Amir's half-brother.*

The narrative presents more evidence of the brutality of the Taliban, especially in relation to the Hazaras, through Hassan's account of a Talib beating Farzana. The atrocities the Taliban commit re-emerge in Hassan's dreams of 'hanged corpses rotting in soccer fields with blood-red grass' (p.191). This violence culminates in the murder of Hassan and Farzana by the Taliban. The reason that the Taliban give for this murder is that Hassan is 'a liar and a thief like all Hazaras' (p.192).

Rahim Khan's view of Amir is more positive than Baba's and the reader now sees Amir in a different light. Amir supposes that this is because Rahim Khan 'always thought too highly of [him]' (p.194), but Rahim Khan tells him that he has always been too hard on himself.

Q Whose judgment of Amir's character is closer to the truth in your view, Rahim Khan's or Baba's?

Eighteen (pp.196–9)

Summary: *Amir reflects on Baba's lies; he decides to go to Kabul to bring back Sohrab.*

Key point

In learning that Hassan was Baba's illegitimate son, Amir is forced to re-evaluate his opinion of his father. He now sees a connection between his father and himself, but it is not an honourable one: 'We had both betrayed the people who would have given their lives for us' (p.197).

Amir reaches a turning point in his life and chooses to take up the challenge that Rahim Khan gives him of finding forgiveness. Unexpectedly, Amir now needs to atone not only for his own failings but also for his father's.

Q Why did Baba remain silent about Hassan's parentage?

Nineteen (pp.200–12)

Summary: *Amir travels to Kabul with Farid; Farid is dismissive of Amir's return to Afghanistan until he hears about Sohrab; Amir stays with Farid's brother and sister-in-law overnight.*

Key scene

Amir is driven to Kabul by Farid, an ethnic Tajik, whose attitude towards Amir is initially disdainful. Farid contrasts Amir's privileged upbringing with his own experience of an Afghanistan marked by poverty and hard work. Farid says: "That's the real Afghanistan, Agha sahib. That's the Afghanistan I know. You? You've *always* been a tourist here, you just didn't know it" (p.204). This scene raises some important issues in relation to the narrator's point of view. Hosseini asks the reader to compare Amir's experience of life in a wealthy suburb of Kabul with the conditions that his fellow Afghans live in. We see that Amir's understanding of Afghanistan is limited to his own experience and that many other perspectives on life in Afghanistan exist beyond his own.

The hospitality of Farid's brother and his family comes at some expense to themselves but, again, hospitality is a highly valued trait in Afghan culture. Perhaps through this experience, and through his efforts to atone for his past, Amir begins to reconnect with Afghanistan and to feel a 'kinship' with his country.

Q Do you agree that Amir has always been a tourist in his own country?

Twenty (pp.213–25)

Summary: *Amir returns to Kabul to find it is in ruins and that the Taliban patrol the streets; Amir goes to the orphanage to find Sohrab but discovers he has been 'bought'.*

Farid warns Amir that Kabul is not how he remembers it, but this does not prepare him for the sight of beggars on almost every street corner and the constant presence of the Taliban. The Taliban whom Amir sees are nicknamed the 'Beard Patrol' by Farid because of their strict enforcement of the Muslim custom of wearing a beard. It is in order to be overlooked by these patrols that Amir buys a false beard while he is in Pakistan (p.202).

Zaman, the director of the relocated orphanage, is one of the most morally corrupt characters in the text. He has 'sold' Sohrab to a member of the Taliban, but he rationalises his actions by saying that if he didn't sell the children they would be taken anyway.

Q Look at Zaman's explanation for his actions on page 224. Do you think there is some justification for what he does? Do you think that Amir disapproves of Zaman as much as Farid does?

Twenty-one (pp.226–38)

Summary: *Amir returns to his old neighbourhood, which is now occupied by the Taliban and the people backing them; Farid and Amir stay in a run-down hotel in Kabul; they attend a football match where a man and a woman are stoned to death in punishment for adultery.*

Key point

Amir makes an important decision when he returns to his old neighbourhood: he does not want to forget any more. His journey to Kabul to redeem himself is already successful in that he is willing to face his past, rather than let it haunt him through nightmares and an overwhelming sense of guilt.

Evidence of the Taliban's cruelty and violence abound in this chapter, which opens with the scene of a young man's dead body hanging from a tree. The Taliban punishments are so common in Kabul that even a sight such as this becomes an everyday occurrence: 'Hardly anyone seemed to notice [the body]' (p.226). The Afghans are so impoverished that Amir witnesses a man trying to sell his artificial leg in order to obtain money to feed his family.

This may seem extraordinary, but it is worth remembering that Afghanistan has one of the greatest concentrations of landmines of any country in the world, and many Afghans have lost limbs in landmine explosions.

The chapter ends with the grim scene of a public execution by stoning at a football match. Amir arranges to meet the executioner, who has also 'bought' Sohrab.

Q Why was it important for Amir to return to Kabul?

Twenty-two (pp.239–55)

Summary: *Amir meets the executioner who is revealed to be Assef; Assef beats Amir but Sohrab uses his slingshot to blind him; Sohrab and Farid assist the wounded Amir out of Assef's house.*

Key scene

Amir feels that he is acting out of character in going to the Taliban official's house: 'This isn't you, Amir, part of me said. You're gutless. It's how you were made' (p.240). Nevertheless, he persists with his quest to retrieve Sohrab. The Taliban official is probably a heroin user – 'I saw marks on his forearm – I'd seen those same tracks on homeless people living in grimy alleys in San Francisco' (p.241) – and he admits to being amongst the Taliban who massacred the Hazaras in 1998.

In tearing off Amir's false beard and revealing himself to be Amir's childhood enemy, Assef recreates the grounds for a confrontation that Amir avoided when he was young. The scene that has haunted Amir from his childhood, in which he failed to stand up to Assef and deserted Hassan, is reproduced here and Amir has the chance to redeem himself by protecting Sohrab. Hosseini emphasises the similarities between the two scenes by using the same sacrificial lamb imagery that was used in describing Hassan's rape. In protecting Sohrab, Amir also saves himself: 'for the first time since the winter of 1975, I felt at peace' (p.253).

Q Is Amir still as 'gutless' as he thinks he is?

Twenty-three (pp.256–70)

Summary: *Amir recovers in hospital in Peshawar, Pakistan; he reads Rahim Khan's letter.*

Amir is seriously injured and delirious for part of the time that he is in hospital. As he is recovering he reads the letter from Rahim Khan. The letter helps Amir to reconcile himself to his own history. Rahim Khan points out the benefits of conscience and atonement for the past; he also explains something of Baba's attempt to redeem himself by building the orphanage.

Q What do you make of Amir's dream, where Assef says "you're my twin" (p.268)?

Q Amir includes many of his dreams in his narrative; how much light do they shed on the events or ideas in the text?

Twenty-four (pp.271–99)

Summary: *Amir goes to Islamabad with Sohrab; Sohrab runs away to the mosque; Amir asks Sohrab to come to America; he asks for help from the American Embassy; Sohrab attempts suicide.*

Sohrab reveals to Amir that he feels "dirty and full of sin" (p.278) because he has been sexually abused by Assef and the two followers. In reassuring him, Amir feels that there is a bond between them, like the one that existed between Amir and Hassan.

Soraya agrees that Sohrab should come to America and be adopted by them since Sohrab is Amir's *qaom* (p.284). Amir has more difficulty, however, convincing the American consular official, Raymond Andrews, that Sohrab should be allowed to live in America. Without the assistance of a relative who has some influence with migration processes it seems that Sohrab would not be able to migrate to America. Amir breaks his promise to Sohrab and suggests that he goes to an orphanage in Pakistan until migration can be arranged.

Q Was Amir justified in breaking his promise to Sohrab?

Twenty-five (pp.300–24)

Summary: *Sohrab recovers in the intensive care unit; in August 2001 Sohrab and Amir arrive in America; Soraya and Amir become involved in Afghan projects; Sohrab remains silent; in March 2002, Amir runs a kite for Sohrab.*

When Sohrab attempts suicide Amir finally decides that there must be a God, and that he will pray to him for Sohrab's life. This is a very important decision for Amir and it comes at the end of a lifetime of vacillation between his father's lack of belief in God and what he has been taught by the mullahs.

Sohrab's presence in Amir's household causes some tension between General Taheri and his daughter. It is an indication of the growth of Amir's character that he is able to tell the truth about Sohrab's parentage to the General and also, for the first time, to speak out against discrimination against Hazaras. Amir tells the General: "You will never again refer to him as 'Hazara boy' in my presence. He has a name and it's Sohrab" (p.315).

World events quickly intrude into the lives of Amir and his small family with the destruction of the World Trade Centre on 11 September 2001 and, in December, the beginning of talks to elect a government in Afghanistan.

The text ends with a return to kite fighting and a reversal of roles for Amir as he becomes a kite runner for Sohrab, thus taking Hassan's place. At this moment there is a glimmer of hope that Sohrab will begin to engage with life again and take an active role in his new family.

Q Do you think that Sohrab will recover? This question is well suited to a discussion: make sure you support your point of view with references to the text.

CHARACTERS & RELATIONSHIPS

Amir

Key quotes

"A boy who won't stand up for himself becomes a man who can't stand up to anything." (Baba about Amir, p.20)
'And that right there was the single greatest moment of my twelve years of life, seeing Baba on that roof, proud of me at last.' (p.58)
"You've always thought too highly of me, Rahim Khan." "And you've always been far too hard on yourself." (p.194)
'This isn't you, Amir, part of me said. You're gutless. It's how you were made. And that's not such a bad thing because your saving grace is that you've never lied to yourself about it.' (pp.240–1)

Amir as narrator

Amir is both the narrator of *The Kite Runner* and its protagonist. He is thus able to give the reader personal insights into events and characters in the text, but he is also limited in his understanding of the other characters and events by the nature of his role as one of the characters. In texts which have an omniscient narrator – that is, a third-person narrator who stands outside the text and knows what has come before and what will happen in the future – the reader is often given a picture of the characters from what must be an infallible source of knowledge.

Far from being infallible and all-knowing, as a man in his late thirties who, as he himself admits, has his own strengths and flaws, Amir has only a partial understanding of other characters and events. His understanding is limited in some cases by his age and his background, and in other cases because information has been kept from him by other characters. A good example of this second kind of limited understanding is that Amir does not know until late in the text that Hassan is his half-brother. Rahim Khan knew that this was the case and so, of course, did Baba, but this information was purposely kept from Amir.

The first-person narration is not a hindrance to the narrative of *The Kite Runner* since dramatic tension builds throughout the text around the elements of the story which Amir is perplexed and frustrated by, such as the unexplained aspects of the relationship between Baba and Hassan.

It does mean, however, that readers need to do some interpretive work to come to their own understanding of Amir. In order to build a picture of Amir, readers must pay close attention to his statements about himself and to what other characters say about him.

Amir as a boy

Key quotes

'That was how I escaped my father's aloofness, in my dead mother's books. That and Hassan, of course.' (p.17)

Key point

One of the driving forces behind Amir's actions is his anxious fight to win his father's approval. Amir senses that there is something missing in his relationship with his father but he is not sure, until he overhears a conversation between Rahim Khan and Baba, what is lacking. He attributes his father's aloofness to the fact that his mother died in giving birth to him; he pins his hopes to winning the kite-fighting contest so that 'I would finally be pardoned for killing my mother' (p.49). While this may be a possible reason for Baba's distance it does not seem very convincing, since neither Baba nor any of the other characters in the text mention Baba blaming Amir for his mother's death.

Amir makes another attempt to explain his father's lack of warmth towards him: he thinks that he is too bookish and unathletic; in short, he does not resemble his father enough. He thinks that his father believes '[r]eal men didn't read poetry – and God forbid they should ever write it! Real men – real boys – played soccer just as Baba had when he had been young' (p.17). This explanation is supported by the conversation he overhears between Baba and Rahim Khan, so the reader can feel fairly sure that this time Amir is right. When Rahim Khan tells Baba that he should be grateful that Amir is healthy, Baba replies: "I know, I know. But he's always buried in those books or shuffling around the house like he's lost in some dream" (p.19). When Rahim Khan supports Amir, Baba retorts: "I wasn't like that at all, and neither were any of the kids I grew up with" (p.19). Amir makes such a little impression on his father that he feels as if he is 'a ghost in this house' (p.49), and he is aware that his father seems, for reasons which he cannot understand, to favour Hassan.

Amir's failure to intervene when Hassan is raped is the most significant event in Amir's life. His cowardice or, worse than that, his desire to save the blue kite rather than Hassan and thereby gain his father's affections, haunts Amir for the rest of his life. The reader's sympathy for Amir is challenged by this episode and those that follow it. Amir not only sacrifices his childhood friend but he also incriminates Hassan in a theft which he fabricates, forcing Hassan and Ali to relinquish their jobs and the only home they have known. Amir is tempted to tell the truth and save Hassan and Ali but his courage fails him.

Amir compounds his cowardice by shifting responsibility onto someone else. As a child he allows Hassan to accept the blame for their pranks and he takes it as a matter of course that he can hide behind his father's status in society. At school he escapes the punishment meted out to the other students because 'my father was rich and everyone knew him, so I was spared the metal rod treatment' (p.80). Even later in life he blames his father for his treatment of Hassan: 'I didn't want to sacrifice for Baba anymore. The last time I had done that, I had damned myself' (p.117).

The reader's sympathy for Amir is not entirely lost, however, since he is honest about his culpability and cowardice and, as Rahim Khan points out, he does have a conscience and a sense of guilt about his actions.

Amir as an adult

The reader's introduction to Amir happens at an important juncture in his life: the moment, as an adult, when he finds a chance to redeem himself for his actions as a child. As an adult, Amir is aware of his limitations, but once Baba dies and he no longer sees himself only as Baba's son, Amir learns that he can take responsibility for his actions. Amir's journey to rescue Sohrab brings its own reward in helping Amir's personal development.

It is a striking part of Amir's story that the major changes that he experiences do not occur in his adolescence but in his adulthood, as a man in his late thirties. It may be that the image he has of his father as a figure of mythic proportions has to be challenged and debunked before he is able to discover his own value. When Amir discovers the secret that his father had kept from him – that Baba was Hassan's biological father – he finds a way to better understand his father. His own failings do not seem so important once he sees that his father had flaws, too: 'Baba and I were more alike than I'd ever known. We had both betrayed the people who would have given their lives for us' (p.197).

Baba

Key quotes

'With me as the glaring exception, my father molded the world around him to his liking. The problem, of course, was that Baba saw the world in black and white. And he got to decide what was black and what was white.' (p.14)
'Baba loved the *idea* of America. It was living in America that gave him an ulcer.' (p.109)
'"What about me, Baba? What am I supposed to do?" I said, my eyes welling up. A look of disgust swept across his rain-soaked face ... "What's going to happen to you, you say? All those years, that's what I was trying to teach you, how to never have to ask that question."' (p.137)

Baba is an awe-inspiring character whose power, in the eyes of his son, seems to be as great as that of any hero in the fables. Amir's description of Baba certainly has elements of fable in it:

> My father was a force of nature, a towering Pashtun specimen with a thick beard, a wayward crop of curly brown hair as unruly as the man himself, hands that looked capable of uprooting a willow tree, and a black glare that would "drop the devil to his knees begging for mercy," as Rahim Khan used to say. (p.11)

It is not only Amir's impression that Baba is 'a force of nature'; Baba's nickname, given to him by Rahim Khan, is *Toophan Agha* or Mr Hurricane.

Baba's enormous self-confidence allows him to go against prevailing orthodoxy and to question authority in a way that seems incredible to Amir. When Amir tells his father that the mullah has taught him it is sinful to drink alcohol, Baba delivers a colourful curse not just against Amir's mullah but "all of them", telling Amir that he will "never learn anything from those bearded idiots" and prophetically declaring: "God help us all if Afghanistan ever falls into their hands" (p.15). Baba's challenge to the Russian border guard (p.100) is another good example of his willingness to challenge authority and defend his own moral convictions in the face of overwhelming odds.

It is clear that Baba's character contrasts markedly with the more passive and introverted Amir, and this is a great source of embarrassment to Baba. Baba protests to Rahim Khan about Amir's reaction to the death at the *Buzkashi* game and his generally bookish demeanour: "I wasn't like that at all, and neither were any of the kids I grew up with" (p.19). He is also baffled by Amir's pacifism: "I see him playing on the street with the neighbourhood boys. I see how they push him around ... he never fights back ... There's something missing in that boy" (p.20). Baba is disappointed with Amir because he cannot see himself reflected in his son and it is, instead, the illegitimate son, Hassan, who more closely resembles Baba in his courage and athleticism.

Baba's power wanes when he moves to America, however. Although he is essentially the same man, with the same set of values that he has always had, his context changes and his values are no longer the norm in the broader society. Baba rejects the food stamps offered to political refugees because he sees them as a slight to Pashtun pride, yet we learn later in the text that General Taheri, another significant Pashtun character, lives on government assistance. Hosseini suggests that Baba's pride, while having a great deal to do with appearances, is deeper than that; it is certainly greater than that of his nearest Afghan contemporary in America. As Baba grows older in another culture his influence diminishes, and he finds himself being forced to conform to rules which, he feels, undermine his stature. When Baba is asked to show identification in order to cash a cheque at the local grocery store he is outraged, but it is the outrage of someone who is powerless, and the roles of father and son are reversed when Amir has to come to his rescue.

This is not to say that Baba loses his charismatic power entirely. When Amir graduates from high school, Baba turns an evening at the local bar into a celebration: 'When we left, everyone was sad to see him go. Kabul, Peshawar, Hayward. Same old Baba, I thought, smiling' (p.116). Baba's sense of his own strength does not diminish; even with the prospect of death in front of him he maintains his independence of thought, telling his doctor that there would be "no chemo medication for me", maintaining as he says it 'the same resolved look on his face as the day he'd dropped the stack of food stamps on Mrs. Dobbins's desk' (p.136).

Eventually, after Baba's death, we learn of the secret that he had kept throughout his life – that he is Hassan's father. The fact that Baba has kept his relationship to Hassan secret indicates his shame about fathering an illegitimate child and the great value Baba places on appearances. Rahim Khan acknowledges that it was "a shameful situation" and he explains the shame in the context of Afghan culture: "People would talk. All that a man had then, all that he was, was his honor, his name, and if people talked ...' (p.195).

In some ways, Baba's refusal to admit his paternity of Hassan is uncharacteristically conventional. We might expect that Baba's habit of nonconformity, his maverick status, would lead to an admission that Hassan was his son. However, the force of social convention and *Pashtunwali* in this instance is stronger than Baba's sense of his own individual identity. The differentiating factor here is that Baba has crossed a number of social and cultural taboos in fathering Hassan, and in order to admit that Hassan was his son he would need to broach the even stronger prejudice against Hazaras.

Hassan

Key quotes

'And that's the thing about people who mean everything they say. They think everyone else does too.' (p.48)

'"Hassan!" I called. "Come back with it!" He was already turning the street corner, his rubber boots kicking up snow. He stopped, turned. He cupped his hands around his mouth. "For you a thousand times over!" he said.' (p.59)

'Everywhere I turned, I saw signs of his loyalty, his goddamn unwavering loyalty.' (p.78)

Hassan is a product of his background: he is an ethnic Hazara and a Shi'a Muslim; Hassan is, like Ali, a servant in Baba's household. Because of his background Hassan, although very intelligent, is unable to read and not expected to have any education. He is destined to be a servant, just as Ali was, yet he has a close companion in Amir, nominally his master.

Part of the power of this text lies in the overturning of the expectations of Hassan's role in life. Hassan does manage to learn to read; he deals with Amir's problems with tact and subtlety and, when he leaves Baba's house, he starts his own family and lives an independent life.

Hassan's goodness and intelligence and his devotion to Amir, are qualities which are apparent to the reader from the beginning of the text. Ironically, these good qualities, especially his attachment Amir, are the cause of his greatest suffering. Hassan willingly accepts blame for childish pranks that Amir instigates, he protects Amir from the neighbourhood bullies and, finally, he allows himself to be accused of theft in order to protect Amir from his father's wrath. The metaphor that accompanies many descriptions of Hassan is that of the sacrificial lamb, and the narrator intends the reader to view Hassan's actions and, indeed, much of his life as selfless and dedicated to the good of others. (See the 'Language' section for more discussion of this image.)

The rape of Hassan by Assef is the crisis at the centre of the text and it is the event that haunts Amir throughout his life. Hassan is greatly damaged by this experience, but the incident that causes him to change his life completely and leave his childhood home is not the rape but Amir's betrayal. When Amir plots to have Hassan dismissed for theft by hiding his own watch and money under Hassan's mattress, his treachery is more than Hassan can tolerate, and it is then that Ali and Hassan make the decision to leave Baba's house.

Once Hassan leaves Kabul he drops out of the narrative as an active character, but he lives on for Amir as a constant reminder of his culpability and for Baba as the missing person at their celebrations. Hassan's name becomes a trigger for guilt in Amir:

> Then Baba rolled his head toward me. "I wish Hassan had been with us today," he said.

> A pair of steel hands closed around my windpipe at the sound of Hassan's name. I rolled down the window. Waited for the steel hands to loosen their grip. (p.116)

Hassan's absence is, in a way, as powerful as his presence in reminding both father and son of the wrongs that they have left unresolved in Afghanistan.

Hassan figures prominently in Rahim Khan's narrative (chapter sixteen). Rahim Khan, the trusted narrator, endorses Hassan's generosity when he tells Amir that Hassan rescued him from loneliness by selflessly returning to Kabul with him. Rahim Khan also represents Hassan as intelligent and more perceptive than most people since he knows that the Taliban are dangerous. When the rest of Kabul is celebrating their arrival in the city and the country's deliverance from the Mujahedin, Hassan shakes his head, saying: "God help the Hazaras now" (p.186). His words echo those of Baba who had presciently said: "God help us all if Afghanistan ever falls into [the mullahs'] hands" (p.15).

While Hassan does not appear in the text with Amir again after he leaves Baba's house, he is still influential, both through Rahim Khan's account and through his own letters to Amir. Hosseini has written the character of Hassan so that he represents, or is the 'face' of, Afghanistan in Amir's eyes. While Hassan's fate is, like Afghanistan's, to be mistreated, Hosseini suggests that reparation can be made for the wrongs committed against both Hassan and Afghanistan, even if that happens in the next generation.

Rahim Khan

Rahim Khan, like Baba and Amir, is a Pashtun Sunni. He is a very loyal person who keeps private the secrets of Baba and Hassan. It is a testament to Rahim Khan's loyalty that he keeps Baba's secret until he is about to die and only then does he reveal the secret as a way of making recompense for the wrongs that Amir, Baba and, to a certain degree, Rahim Khan himself have done.

Rahim Khan is Baba's friend and business partner and the person whom both Baba and Amir trust most. He is the only character in the text who is able to check Baba's rashness or ameliorate some of the harsher criticisms Baba makes of Amir. He is a wise counsellor to Baba and he shows himself to be Baba's equal in being unafraid to say what he thinks. This is well illustrated when he counters Baba's criticism that Amir is nothing like him with the observation that "sometimes you are the most self-centered man I know" (p.19).

Rahim Khan is a mentor to Amir, offering the affection that Baba denies to the lonely boy and encouraging his story writing. A photograph of Baba, Amir and Rahim Khan shows Amir's affection for Rahim Khan: 'Baba is holding me, looking tired and grim. I'm in his arms, but it's Rahim Khan's pinky my fingers are curled around' (p.5).

This affectionate bond is sustained throughout the text, although it is severely strained when Amir learns that Rahim Khan has kept Hassan's real relationship with him secret. It is Amir's love for Rahim Khan that causes Amir to return to Pakistan and later to Afghanistan. Consequently, Rahim Khan is instrumental in Amir's endeavour to overcome his guilt. By leaving Sohrab's fate in Amir's hands, Rahim Khan allows Amir a chance to achieve redemption.

Soraya

Amir meets Soraya at the San Jose flea market. She is a Pashtun and the daughter of Khala Jamila and General Taheri, whom Baba describes as "a Pashtun to the root" (p.126). Soraya is the subject of gossip and conjecture in the Afghan-American community because she had left her parents' house to live with her boyfriend. This behaviour has disgraced her in the eyes of her community and her standing in the community is devalued: she is seen as 'an unwed young woman. One with a *history*, no less' (p.128). Amir explains that because Soraya is a woman, the weight of disapproval falls squarely upon her. He knows that his speaking to her in public will lead to her being the subject of gossip: 'Poison tongues would flap. And she would bear the brunt of that poison, not me' (p.128). When Amir marries Soraya, Khala Jamila is relieved of 'the greatest fear of every Afghan mother' (p.155) – that no-one would marry her daughter.

Soraya is instrumental in helping Amir to develop in maturity. She shows him that there is some consolation in speaking about the thing one feels guilty about. Her honesty about her past is an object lesson for Amir: 'I envied her. Her secret was out. Spoken. Dealt with' (p.144). Although Amir does learn from Soraya, he is still unable to confess his own betrayal of Hassan.

Ali and Baba

The relationship between Ali and Baba is, on the surface, what the relationship between Hassan and Amir could have been. Baba and Ali had been companions since childhood and, although Ali is Baba's servant, he is treated with kindness by Baba. Baba reminisces about their shared childhood games with affection, although Ali corrects the impression Baba makes of their carefree, reckless lives by saying that it was Baba who initiated their childhood pranks. This is very much like the relationship between Amir and Hassan and, given the obvious parallels between the two friendships, we would suppose that this might have been the future for Hassan and Amir, should the war and Baba's hidden relationship to Hassan not have intervened.

It is in this concealed relationship between Baba and Hassan that some difficulties arise in understanding how Baba managed to maintain his dignity with Ali. Amir acknowledges, but never attempts to explain, Baba's dishonourable relationship with Ali: he learns only from Rahim Khan that Ali did not know that Baba was Hassan's father.

Assef

Assef is a vicious bully even as a young boy; he intimidates the neighbourhood children, singling out the weakest of them and pummelling them with brass knuckles. Assef is responsible for the most horrifying incidents in the text, raping Hassan and later holding Sohrab captive in his house and abusing him, as he did his father.

The character of Assef does not change as the novel progresses. He remains a bully throughout, but as his power grows his crimes become more heinous. Assef is intended to be an evil character and Hosseini reinforces the malevolence in his character by creating associations with Hitler, who is Assef's hero, and with Mullah Mohammed Omar, the leader of the Taliban. The connection with Hitler is the more obvious one, since Assef subscribes to Hitler's ideologies, even giving Amir a book on Hitler as a birthday present. Assef's disfigurement through the loss of an eye links him to another reviled character, Afghanistan's Mullah Mohammed Omar who, like Assef, has a towering build and only one eye.

Assef is an unwaveringly evil character who is incapable of empathy or change. He seems to take pleasure in the horrific crimes he commits against others, conducting the public execution of a man and woman by stoning them himself and then, without a sign of remorse, going on to a conduct a meeting at his house. Assef does not allow either family or friendship to have any claim on his emotions. He dominates his parents from his early years, so that Amir's wonders if 'maybe, on some level, their son frightened them' (p.84), and Assef's childhood allies follow him more in fear of him than out of friendship.

THEMES & ISSUES

Atonement

Key quotes

'What was so funny was that, for the first time since the winter of 1975, I felt at peace.' (pp.252–3)
'And this is what I want you to understand, that good, real good, was born out of your father's remorse.' (Rahim Khan's letter to Amir, p. 263)

Atonement is an important idea in *The Kite Runner* since, in making reparation for his betrayal of Hassan, Amir can forgive himself and find the courage to declare that Hassan is his half-brother. The first step in atoning for the wrongs one has committed is, as Rahim Khan tells Amir, in feeling remorse for one's actions. Unlike Assef, who has no feelings of guilt or remorse whatsoever, Amir does acknowledge that he has done the wrong thing. In fact he feels so guilty that his life is overshadowed by the mistakes he made as a child.

Amir is tortured by his guilt partly because he does not admit his crimes to anyone. His guilt is fed by the secrecy with which he surrounds his past. He makes a half-hearted attempt to tell someone else about what he has done by whispering his secret to the sleeping adults at Jalalabad, but he knows that no-one hears him and so he continues to suffer.

Amir understands the burden of secrecy well enough to envy Soraya's ability to talk about her past, realising that it is a way of acquiring some peace of mind. It is not until he meets Rahim Khan again, however, that his secret comes into the open and he then is free to move to the next stage and atone for his crimes against Hassan.

Amir's atonement does not happen at once. His guilt does not go away, as Rahim Khan told him it would, when he successfully rescues Sohrab, but it does when Amir confronts Assef. When Assef brutally beats Amir, as he has been threatening to do since they were children, Amir begins to laugh because, he says, he feels 'at peace' (p.253). In opposing Assef, Amir finds he has made amends for betraying Hassan. It is the process of making atonement, Hosseini suggests, which brings an individual peace of mind. That process involves, first of all, feeling guilt and admitting to the past wrongdoing and then setting about making amends for that wrong.

Sacrifice

Key quotes

"But before you sacrifice yourself for him, think about this: Would he do the same for you?" (Assef, pp.63–4)
'Maybe Hassan was the price I had to pay, the lamb I had to slay to win Baba.' (p.68)
'Then I understood: This was Hassan's final sacrifice for me.' (p.91)

Amir's experience of sacrifice is most often linked to Hassan. Because Hassan is innocent and guileless the image of a lamb is linked to him in Amir's mind. Hassan does, indeed, make sacrifices for Amir; accepting the blame for shining mirrors into neighbours' houses and standing up to the local bullies. Amir believes Hassan sacrifices himself so that Amir will keep the blue kite, and Hassan also allows himself to be falsely accused of theft in order to spare Amir from his father's anger and rejection.

Amir's guilt about Hassan's rape means that his horror of the idea of a sacrificial lamb continues throughout his life, despite the fact that *nazr* is an important ceremony in his community. He pleads with his mother-in-law to abandon the practice for him: "Please, no *nazr*, Khala jan ... No sheep killing" (p.159).

Friendship

The idea of friendship in this text has a great deal of weight attached to it. Friendship means something quite specific to the characters, and it is a term that neither Amir nor Baba confers on a relationship without serious consideration. While it is clear that Rahim Khan and Baba are friends – Amir refers to Rahim Khan as Baba's 'best friend' (p.5) – other friendships seem qualified and remote. There is considerable social activity in the extended family circles in Afghanistan and in the newly formed *qaoms* in America, but the friendships that the text depicts carry an extra burden.

Amir admits that he 'never thought of Hassan and [himself] as friends' (p.22), despite their growing up in the same house and spending almost all their free time playing together. While Hassan sees himself and Amir as friends, the older Amir, who narrates the childhood scenes retrospectively, is adamant that there could be no friendship between himself and Hassan because of the cultural and religious differences that separate them: 'I was a Pashtun and he was a Hazara, I was Sunni and he was Shi'a, and nothing was ever going to change that' (p.22).

In the friendship between Baba and Rahim Khan there is a great deal of reciprocity – Rahim Khan is allowed to make disparaging remarks about Baba's egotistical behaviour and to defend Amir when he is being criticised because of the depth of the friendship that exists between the two men. Friendship, as Hosseini represents it, flourishes among people who see themselves as equals, who have equal power and privilege and who share common cultural values. Rahim Khan and Baba are friends because they are on an equal economic footing – they are business partners – as well as an equal social and cultural footing. They are both wealthy, privileged members of the Pashtun ethnic group living in Kabul.

There is another element to the friendship between Baba and Rahim Khan: they share confidences with one another. Rahim Khan is the only person who can verify the fact that Hassan is Baba's son; he is the only person whom Baba has trusted with what he sees as a shameful fact.

Gender and ethnicity

Key quotes

"I cringed a little at the position of power I'd been granted, and all because I had won at the genetic lottery that had determined my sex.' (p.130)
"He handed me a pair of scissors and calmly told me to cut off all my hair. He watched while I did it." (Soraya, p.156)
'"In the west, they have an expression for that," I said. "They call it ethnic cleansing." "Do they?" Assef's face brightened. "Ethnic cleansing. I like it. I like the sound of it."' (p.249)

Ethnicity and gender are the central sources of discrimination in *The Kite Runner*. In the Afghan community there is a definite hierarchy in ethnic background and in gender, with Pashtuns occupying the privileged position among all ethnic groups and males being the privileged sex. Hosseini explores both these hierarchies in a number of ways.

Firstly, Amir, the central character, is a male Pashtun, and therefore he occupies a highly privileged position. Amir makes direct comments on the position of power conferred upon him because of his birth, when he 'won at the genetic lottery' (p.130). He also despairs for Afghanistan when he repeatedly confronts the inbuilt prejudice against Hazaras. He thinks that 'maybe what people said about Afghanistan was true. Maybe it *was* a hopeless place' (p.233), when Farid casually dismisses Sohrab because he is a Shi'a.

The second way that Hosseini explores discrimination in the text is through the stories that the other characters tell. Soraya's experience of the double standards that affect Afghan women is conveyed through her conversations with Amir. Soraya angrily derides the double standard that allows Afghan boys so much sexual freedom yet condemns her after one sexual experience: "I have to have my face rubbed in it for the rest of my life" (p.156). She also tells Amir about her father handing her a pair of scissors and forcing her to cut off all her hair; a traditional humiliation for women who have transgressed the customs of the society.

The ideas of ethnicity and discrimination are explored largely through the characters of Hassan and Ali who are ethnic Hazaras. Hosseini frames the particular stories of Hassan and Ali in the general context of a missing history of the Hazaras, and paints a picture of a bias against them that is so entrenched that discrimination is the first reaction for most of the characters in the text.

The history of the Hazaras had been suppressed in the school books that Amir reads, but his mother's history book points out the long-standing animosity between the Pashtuns, Amir's ethnic group, and the Hazaras, Hassan's ethnic group. He learns that one of the reasons for the oppression of the Hazaras was that they were Shi'a Muslims, whereas the Pashtuns were Sunnis. When Amir draws his teacher's attention to this book he runs up against the same kind of prejudice he finds elsewhere in Afghanistan: the teacher 'wrinkled up his nose when he said the word Shi'a, like it was some kind of disease' (p.8).

The reader gains some insight into the way that books can offer an alternative view to the one that is available in mainstream education and culture. In this instance they provide Amir with an opportunity for developing ideas that question commonly held prejudices. Amir does not appear to be bigoted as a child, but the information he gleans from reading his mother's books supports his instinctive friendship with Hassan and, more broadly, helps him develop a different world view from many other characters in the text.

The existence of God

Key quotes

'"God is going to save us all. Why don't you pray to him?" Baba snorted a pinch of his snuff. Stretched his legs. "What'll save us is eight cylinders and a good carburettor." That silenced the rest of them for good about the matter of God.' (p.104)

'That night, I waited until Baba fell asleep, and then folded a blanket. I used it as a prayer rug ... and asked for kindness from a God I wasn't sure existed. I envied the mullah now, envied his faith and certainty.' (p.135)

'I see now that Baba was wrong, there is a God, there always had been. I see Him here, in the eyes of the people in this corridor of desperation.' (p.301)

Hosseini examines the idea of the existence of God through two major characters in the text, Baba and Amir. Baba does not believe there is a God, whereas Amir is agnostic at the beginning of the text but becomes a believer by the end.

Baba's view about the existence of God is consistent with his fiercely independent character. He feels that you must rely on yourself rather than asking God to provide for you. Baba's point of view is very unconventional and runs against the mainstream culture of Afghanistan, yet he manages to sustain his atheism because of his own power and influence: 'Baba saw the world in black and white. And he got to decide what was black and what was white' (p.14). Baba is able to hold this view because of the times he lived in. During the king's reign, his views could be tolerated or ignored because of the relative liberalism of the era. Baba's habit of living his life according to his own rules was permitted because the society he lived in did not punish individuals for dissenting against the mainstream culture, as long as that dissent was private.

The real object of Baba's rage is not religious belief itself, but the mullahs. When Amir tells him that the mullahs disapprove of drinking alcohol, Baba lets it be known that he thinks their opinions are worthless: they are, in his opinion, "bearded idiots" (p.15).

Amir is undecided about the existence of God until he comes to a crisis in his life. When Baba is dying he looks for some reassurance through prayer and he envies the mullahs' certainty. From this time, Amir becomes increasingly religious, beginning with prayers that are half-remembered from childhood and finally becoming a devout Muslim. Ironically, Amir's growing faith in God gives him the same critical perspective on the Taliban's moral police that Baba would have had. Amir is critical of the Taliban because in enforcing strict Islamic customs they undermine the tenets of Islam and he sees their notion of justice as indefensible.

Father–son relationships

Key quotes

'By the end of summer, the scraping of spoon and fork against the plate had replaced dinner table chatter and Baba had resumed retreating to his study after supper. And closing the door.' (p.81)
'I wondered if maybe, on some level, their son frightened them.' (pp.83–4)
"Don't you challenge me in public, Amir. Ever. Who do you think you are?" (p.136)

The relationship between father and son is a basic focus in literature. One of the defining characteristics of this relationship is that the father has the ultimate power in the dealings between father and son. How the father chooses to exercise that power and the reactions of the son to being subjugated to his father's control are variables which change with individual relationships. In *The Kite Runner*, Baba's aloof style of parenting contrasts with Ali's affectionate, yet not indulgent, treatment of Hassan. Baba's relationship with Hassan, who we learn is Baba's son by birth, is more 'fatherly' than the relationship he has with Amir during his childhood.

In Afghanistan the relationship between father and son has its own complexities, since Afghan society is a patriarchal one. Here fatherhood is a revered institution and one of the foundation stones of that society. Hosseini has suggested in an interview that in Afghan society 'You have your mother's love, but you earn your father's'.[4] This reverence for fatherhood means that the relationship between son and father is, in general, more removed and distant, characterised by respect and adherence to an established etiquette.

Hosseini presents a number of relationships between father and son in the text and he also explores the idea of the absence of fatherhood. Amir and Soraya's inability to have a child is an overwhelmingly important issue for them both, and the fact of their childlessness emphasises further the importance of fatherhood. Amir feels that his fatherless state is somehow pre-ordained because of his treatment of Hassan: 'perhaps something, someone, somewhere, had decided to deny me fatherhood for the things I had done' (p.164).

Baba and Amir

Key quotes

'I was always learning things about Baba from other people.' (p.16)

Amir is a disappointment to Baba, because Baba feels that Amir does not mirror his own qualities of dynamism, strength and athleticism. Baba makes a crushing observation about Amir, "If I hadn't seen the doctor pull him out of my wife with my own eyes, I'd never believe he's my son" (p.20). Amir knows that he is a disappointment to his father, not only because he overhears his father saying so, but because Baba maintains a cool reserve in his dealings with his son. Amir's reaction to this treatment is at once puzzled and ambivalent. Amir 'wanted to be just like Baba' and, at the same time, he 'wanted to be nothing like him' (p.160).

4 Khaled Hosseini, interview with Liane Hansen broadcast on National Public Radio, 27 July 2003, http://www.npr.org/templates/story/story.php?storyId=1358775

The affection which develops between Baba and Amir grows as Baba grows older and the difference in their status lessens. Amir reflects:

> Maybe that was why Baba and I had been on such better terms in the U.S. ... Selling junk for petty cash, our menial jobs, our grimy apartment – the American version of a hut. (p.264)

Hosseini leaves the reader wondering if Baba's death provides some sort of release for Amir. In the future Amir may not be defined by his relationship to Baba, but may find his identity on his own terms. Listening to the mourners at Baba's funeral, Amir again comes to understand something vital about his relationship with his father:

> I realized how much of who I was, what I was, had been defined by Baba ... I had been "Baba's son." Now he was gone. Baba couldn't show me the way anymore; I'd have to find it on my own. (p.152)

A resolution to the conflicts in the relationship comes through the wisdom of Rahim Khan, who points out the similarities, painful though it may be for Amir to recognise them, between Amir and Baba: "Your father, like you, was a tortured soul, Amir jan" (p.263).

The heroic father

We have already noted that the description of Baba in the chapters set in Afghanistan is very close to a description of a hero in a folk tale or a fable. When Baba snores it is 'like a growling truck engine' (p.12), and Amir thinks that his legs are like 'tree trunks' (p.14). Like a hero in a fable, Baba defeats a wild bear by wrestling with it. He also takes on any opposition in the community and turns it into a commendation of his efforts:

> Skeptics had urged him to stop his foolishness and hire an architect. Of course, Baba refused, and everyone shook their heads in dismay at his obstinate ways. Then Baba succeeded and everyone shook their heads in awe at his triumphant ways. (p.12)

Baba's larger-than-life stature is confirmed by the opinion of other characters in the novel, but it is important to understand that Baba seems so heroic to Amir because Amir sees himself as so unheroic. It is the contrast between father and son that is at the heart of the tension in their relationship, and the more Amir magnifies his father's qualities, the more diminished he seems by comparison. Since Amir casts Baba as the heroic father he must see himself as a lesser character.

We can place the Rostam and Sohrab fable that is the favourite story of Amir and Hassan in this context. Rostam mortally wounds Sohrab in battle, and only then to discover that Sohrab is his son. The sad irony of the story is that Sohrab had been searching for his father's love and Rostam is grief-stricken at having murdered his son. Amir interprets this story not as a tragedy but as a truism: 'didn't all fathers in their secret hearts harbor a desire to kill their sons?' (p.26). The extent of the disconnection between Amir and his apparently heartless father is clear in Amir's remark.

It is not until Amir and Baba move to America and the differences between them become less pronounced that the relationship becomes closer. Amir is at last able to see his father as something other than a heroic figure and himself as more than an unacceptable son. The image that Amir carries of Baba to Pakistan is one of an ageing, frail man in a shiny brown suit. Amir's sense of himself as capable and useful increases in inverse proportion to his father's growing frailty and it may be this growing sense that he is different from his father that allows Amir to accept Rahim Khan's challenge to be 'good again'.

America and Afghanistan

Key quotes

"That's the real Afghanistan, Agha sahib. That's the Afghanistan I know. You? You've *always* been a tourist here, you just didn't know it." (Farid, p.204)

'I stayed awake ... thinking that maybe what people said about Afghanistan was true. Maybe it *was* a hopeless place.' (p.233

The relationship between the United States and Afghanistan has been, and continues to be, a complex and fraught one. This relationship has become even more complicated by the events of 11 September 2001. Afghanistan became a focus for the anger that Americans felt about the attacks on the US because Afghanistan gave refuge to Osama bin Laden, who orchestrated the attacks. As American reprisals against Afghanistan took place, the country suffered greatly under the onslaught.

It is one of the extraordinary features of this text that a novel set mostly in Afghanistan and written by an Afghan writer has become a bestseller in America. One explanation for the text's popularity is that Afghanistan was a little-known country until it came sharply into focus in the late twentieth century, and people from the Western world are curious about life in a country that has brought phrases like 'Mujahedin', 'Taliban' and 'mullah' into our vocabulary.

It is worth looking closely at the views that Hosseini communicates to the reader about both America and Afghanistan in order to understand some underlying issues in the text, such as guilt, memory and the importance of one's own heritage. Amir characterises America as a river of forgetfulness, but knows that his father sees it differently: 'For me, America was a place to bury my memories. For Baba, a place to mourn his' (p.112).

Indeed, Amir embraces America and its exported culture long before he seeks refuge in America. As children, Amir and Hassan spend many hours watching American westerns at the cinema, idolising their heroes, John Wayne and Charles Bronson, and watching their favourite movie, *The Magnificent Seven,* thirteen times. At this stage Amir has little understanding of America, but the influence of its culture is strong in his life. Amir drinks Coca Cola and his father drives a black Mustang, just like Steve McQueen's in *Bullitt*. Amir describes the Americans whom he sees as a child as 'the friendly, long-haired men and women we always saw hanging around in Kabul, dressed in their tattered, brightly colored shirts' (p.23).

Amir's view of America expands beyond its exported culture when he finds refuge in the new country, which offers him a chance to forget painful memories:

> America was different. America was a river, roaring along, unmindful of the past. I could wade into this river, let my sins drown to the bottom, let the waters carry me someplace far. Someplace with no ghosts, no memories, and no sins.
>
> If for nothing else, for that, I embraced America. (p.119)

Important secondary characters in the text endorse Amir's positive view of America. On his return to Pakistan, Rahim Khan notices the positive changes in Amir, remarking: "I see America has infused you with the optimism that has made her so great" (p.176).

It is worth keeping in mind that Hosseini's novel deals with redemption, and the redemption that he explores necessitates confronting the past and making reparation for old sins. In that sense, the refuge America provides is really an interval in the development of the main character, Amir, and the refuge, while it is beneficial in the short term, is not a sustainable way of living. While remaining uncritical of America, Hosseini's observations make it clear that something is seriously out of balance when poverty and great wealth sit side by side and, by implication, we can detect that something is owed by a country of such privilege to other countries which are less fortunate. Amir connects the disjunctions between America and Afghanistan, the past and the present, when he drives through the wealthy suburb of Los Altos:

> I drove past tree-shaded parks that smelled like bark, past strip malls big enough to hold five simultaneous *Buzkashi* tournaments. I drove the Torino up the hills of Los Altos, idling past estates with picture windows and silver lions guarding the wrought-iron gates, homes with cherub fountains lining the manicured walkways and no Ford Torinos in the driveways. Homes that made Baba's house in Wazir Akbar Khan look like a servant's hut. (p.118)

The reference to 'a servant's hut' brings to mind the other great inequality in the text, which is the Hassan's poverty, living in his father's hut in the same grounds as Baba's opulent house.

Although *The Kite Runner* is not allegorical, Hosseini does make some strong connections between Amir and the new world of America, and between Hassan and Afghanistan. Amir 'embraced America', and Hosseini clearly identifies the close connection between Hassan and Afghanistan:

> the face of Afghanistan is that of a boy with a thin-boned frame, a shaved head, and low-set ears, a boy with a Chinese doll face perpetually lit by a harelipped smile. (p.22)

Amir's departure from Afghanistan is a source of his guilt. It is also resented by some of the Afghans who remained in their country during its violent political upheavals, whom he later meets. Amir does embrace the idea of being 'unmindful of the past' in America but he comes back to Afghanistan because reparation must be made. Hosseini draws a parallel between Amir's retreat and the fate of Afghanistan in an interview with *The Providence Journal*:

> I tried to make a statement larger than what was going on in the book. What happened after the Soviet war is that the world just kind of packed its bags and went home and watched as the Afghans were brutalised".[5]

Hosseini has also said

> Afghanistan still needs the long-term international commitment and so on. So if it [*The Kite Runner*] achieves anything toward that end in even a small way, I think it will have been worthwhile'.[6]

5 'Kite Runner author in East Bay', *The Providence Journal*, 6 May 2005, p.CO1.

6 Khaled Hosseini, interview with Liane Hansen broadcast on National Public Radio, 27 July 2003, http://www.npr.org/templates/story/story.php?storyId=1358775.

QUESTIONS & ANSWERS

This section focuses on your own analytical writing on the text, and gives you strategies for producing high quality responses in your coursework and exam essays.

Essay writing – an overview

An essay on a literary work is a formal and serious piece of writing that presents your point of view on the text, usually in response to a given essay topic. Your 'point of view' in an essay is your interpretation of the meaning of the text's language, structure, characters, situations and events, supported by detailed analysis of textual evidence.

Analyse – don't summarise

In your essays it is important to avoid simply summarising what happens in a text.

- A **summary** is a description or paraphrase (retelling in different words) of the characters and events. For example: 'Macbeth has a horrifying vision of a dagger dripping with blood before he goes to murder King Duncan.'
- An **analysis** is an explanation of the real meaning or significance that lies 'beneath' the text's words (and images, for a film). For example: 'Macbeth's vision of a bloody dagger shows how deeply uneasy he is about the violent act he is contemplating – as well as his sense that supernatural forces are impelling him to act.'

A limited amount of summary is sometimes necessary to let your reader know which part of the text you wish to discuss. However, always keep this to a minimum and follow it immediately with your analysis of what this part of the text is really telling us.

Plan your essay

Carefully plan your essay so that you have a clear idea of what you are going to say. The plan ensures that your ideas flow logically, that your argument remains consistent and that you stay on the topic. An essay plan should be a list of **brief dot points** – no more than half a page.

- Include your central argument or main contention – a concise statement (usually in a single sentence) of your overall response to the topic. See 'Analysing a sample topic' for guidelines on how to formulate a main contention.
- Write three or four dot points for each paragraph indicating the main idea and evidence/examples from the text. Note that in your essay you will need to *expand* on these points and *analyse* the evidence.

Structure your essay

An essay is a complete, self-contained piece of writing. It has a clear beginning (the introduction), middle (several body paragraphs) and end (the last paragraph or conclusion). It must also have a central argument that runs throughout, linking each paragraph to form a coherent whole.

See examples of introductions and conclusions in the 'Analysing a sample topic' and 'Sample answer' sections.

The introduction establishes your overall response to the topic. It includes your main contention and outlines the main evidence you will refer to in the course of the essay. Write your introduction *after* you have done a plan and *before* you write the rest of the essay.

The body paragraphs argue your case – they present evidence from the text and explain how this evidence supports your argument. Each body paragraph needs:

- a strong **topic sentence** (usually the first sentence) that states the main point being made in the paragraph
- **evidence** from the text, including some brief quotations
- **analysis** of the textual evidence explaining its significance and **explanation** of how it supports your argument
- **links back to the topic** in one or more statements, usually towards the end of the paragraph.

Connect the body paragraphs so that your discussion flows smoothly. Use some linking words and phrases like 'similarly' and 'on the other hand', though don't start every paragraph like this. Another strategy is to use a significant word from the last sentence of one paragraph in the first sentence of the next.

Use key terms from the topic – or synonyms for them – throughout, so the relevance of your discussion to the topic is always clear.

The conclusion ties everything together and finishes the essay. It includes strong statements that emphasise your central argument and provide a clear response to the topic.

Avoid simply restating the points made earlier in the essay – this will end on a very flat note and imply that you have run out of ideas and vocabulary. The conclusion is meant to be a logical extension of what you have written, not just a repetition or summary. Writing an effective conclusion can be a challenge. Try using these tips:

- Start by linking back to the final sentence of the second-last paragraph – this helps your writing to 'flow', rather than just leaping back to your main contention straight away.
- Use synonyms and expressions with equivalent meanings to vary your vocabulary. This allows you to reinforce your line of argument without being repetitive.
- When planning your essay, think of one or two broad statements or observations about the text's wider meaning. These should be related to the topic and your overall argument. Keep them for the conclusion, since they will give you something 'new' to say but still follow logically from your discussion. The introduction will be focused on the topic, but the conclusion can present a wider view of the text.

Essay topics

1 'Amir is an admirable character not because of his courage in returning to Kabul, but because he is able to be honest about his faults.'
Do you agree?

2 'In rescuing Sohrab, Amir finds redemption not only for himself but for his father.'
Do you agree?

3 'Hassan's good qualities are also the source of his greatest suffering.'
Discuss.

4 'Rahim Khan's friendship is Amir's only refuge in his childhood.'
Do you agree?

5 "Maybe Hassan was the price I had to pay, the lamb I had to slay, to win Baba."
'Despite his efforts, Amir never really succeeds in winning his father's love.'
Do you agree?

6 "And that, I believe, is what true redemption is, Amir jan, when guilt leads to good."
'*The Kite Runner* suggests that individuals can atone for the evil things they have done in their past.'
Discuss.

7 "In the end I was a Pashtun and he was a Hazara, I was Sunni and he was Shi'a, and nothing was ever going to change that."
'*The Kite Runner* argues that inequality breeds brutality.'
Discuss.

8 "But before you sacrifice yourself for him, think about this: Would he do the same for you?"
'*The Kite Runner* suggests that friendship cannot exist when one person is more privileged than another.'
Discuss.

9 '*The Kite Runner* explores the hazards in any relationship that is not between equals, whether that be due to ethnicity, gender, class or power.'
Discuss.

10 '*The Kite Runner* suggests that maturity can only develop with independence.'
Discuss.

Analysing a sample topic

6 "And that, I believe, is what true redemption is, Amir jan, when guilt leads to good." '*The Kite Runner* suggests that individuals can atone for the evil things they have done in their past.'
Discuss.

Before you begin writing the essay

A lot of the hard work in writing an English essay is done before you begin writing. In approaching this topic you will need to look at how ideas like 'guilt', 'good', 'evil' and 'atonement' are built into the text, specifically through the narrator and protagonist, Amir. The question asks you to show how Hosseini's depiction of Amir embodies attitudes to these major ideas.

Once you have defined the terms in the quotation and the contention that accompanies it, you will also need to establish whether you agree or disagree, and to what extent, with the contention. You will then need to think about how you would qualify the statement so that it would better suit your understanding of the values underlying the text.

Writing the essay

In the introduction you should:

- clearly provide your response to the question posed
- locate the quotation in the text
- define any ambiguous terms
- create smooth links between each of these points.

Atonement is possible, Hosseini suggests in *The Kite Runner*, but first the person is in search of redemption must admit guilt. Hosseini explores the ideas of guilt and atonement through Amir, and to a lesser extent through Baba, Amir's father. In his letter to Amir, Rahim Khan attempts to explain the positive value of the guilt that has haunted Amir throughout his life by showing him that it can lead to 'true redemption'.

In the second and third paragraphs you should follow through your claim that the ideas of guilt and atonement are explored through Amir. In supporting your discussion of guilt you could:

- show the debilitating effects of guilt on Amir's life – culminating in his fear that being unable to have a child is his punishment for his childhood actions

- mention his thwarted attempts to confess to Rahim Khan and the sleeping adults at Jalalabad
- contrast Amir's secrecy with Soraya's openness.

When you approach the idea of atonement you will need to continue by showing how Hosseini develops this idea through the development of Amir's character by:

- showing that Amir's growing maturity, partly due to his separation from Baba, allows him to accept the opportunity to atone
- demonstrating that Rahim Khan's position of mentor and trusted friend supports in the reader's mind the validity of his opinions about 'redemption'
- qualifying Amir's notion of completing his task in order to achieve redemption. In confronting Assef, from whom Hassan had shielded him, Amir relives his past cowardice and feels 'healed'. Amir is rescuing Sohrab, but also reliving a past wrongdoing and correcting it.

In the fourth and possibly fifth paragraphs you should show how Baba has made 'atonement' and what he has atoned for. In discussing this second character it is important to make comparisons and contrasts with Amir's journey to atonement. In discussing Baba you should:

- show how his sense of guilt differs from Amir's
- contrast the way Baba confides in Rahim Khan, but still maintains his secret
- demonstrate that his atonement – building the orphanage – while appropriate, was not complete. Amir's quest to bring Sohrab back from Afghanistan is an atonement for the secrets and guilt of all the characters you have discussed: Amir, Baba and Rahim Khan.

In the conclusion you should bring your argument together by stating that the text shows how Amir, despite his guilt and the terrible mistakes he has made, achieves atonement in the process of bringing Sohrab back from Afghanistan and through his confrontation with Assef.

SAMPLE ANSWER

'Baba has all the positive characteristics of bravery, loyalty and success that Amir lacks.' Do you agree?

While the characteristics of bravery and loyalty can certainly be attributed to Baba, it is misleading to state that Amir is lacking in these qualities. For much of *The Kite Runner* Amir is a young boy, and it is clear that many of his actions are motivated above all by loyalty towards his father. Additionally, it is inappropriate to compare Amir's qualities, as well as his level of success, with Baba's in the early parts of the narrative, when Amir's character is still being formed. However, as the narrative progresses Amir comes to achieve success in his own right, although in ways that differ from Baba's own view of what it is to be successful. Moreover, while Baba struggles to maintain the identity he held in Afghanistan, Amir loyally supports and cares for his father, despite the difficulties of their situation as migrants in America. On learning the truth of Hassan's identity, it is Amir who ultimately demonstrates the characteristics of bravery and loyalty through his attempts to rescue and adopt Sohrab.

When the narrative begins, Amir is introduced as an insecure boy who is desperate to secure Baba's love through any means possible. Baba, on the other hand, is a stoic, taciturn character who has 'proved them all wrong' through his remarkable business success and seemingly selfless actions, such as designing and personally funding an orphanage. However, there are several parallels between Amir and Baba. In many cases, Baba's behaviour and attitudes strongly influence the subsequent actions of Amir, such as his treatment of Hassan. While Baba and Ali undoubtedly have a close relationship, 'in none of his stories [does] Baba ever refer to Ali as his friend'; Baba's behaviour towards Ali, and by implication towards the Hazara people in general, thus colours the relationship between Amir and Hassan. Amir believes he treats Hassan 'just like a friend', but then wonders, 'Why did I play with Hassan only when no one else was around?' Moreover, while Baba is seen through a young Amir's eyes as magnanimous, strong and successful, this simplistic view is gradually revised as Amir's self-awareness grows.

In Afghanistan Baba is undoubtedly successful in his career, but he is unable to acknowledge that Amir's talents differ from his own. He expresses his doubts as to Amir's ability to succeed: 'There is something missing in that boy ... I'd never believe he's my son'. Yet, while Baba may have been a successful businessman in Afghanistan, he is unable to fully adapt to life in America, '[scoffing] at the idea' of ESL classes while bemoaning the inadequacy of America when compared with his native Afghanistan. Baba may appear courageous, loyal and successful, but these qualities are only evident when he is immersed in Afghani culture or surrounded by his Afghani friends. It is in fact Amir who demonstrates these character traits in more challenging circumstances. He achieves success as a writer in a new culture and language, and shows courage and loyalty in caring for his father and through his response to Rahim Khan's news about Hassan.

Amir's loyalty is tested in his devotion to Baba; he knows that his betrayal of Hassan was in no small part due to his desperate need to please his father: 'The last time I had [made a sacrifice for Baba], I had damned myself'. Amir's sense of loyalty strengthens as he grows older, though he displays it in a very different way from his father. Baba is always concerned with how others will perceive him; when he learns he has cancer he insists to Amir, 'No one finds out about this, you hear me ... I don't want anybody's sympathy'. He also exhibits a very demonstrative form of courage, as seen in his attempt to protect a young woman from a Russian soldier. Amir silently questions his father's actions, asking 'Do you have to always be the hero?' Moreover, although Baba had cared for Hassan and treated him well, his overriding concern for how he is perceived by others is evident in his refusal to acknowledge that he is Hassan's father. In contrast, when Amir becomes aware of this fact he immediately returns to Afghanistan in search of his brother, and upon learning of his death, sets about finding Sohrab, Hassan's son. Amir's search for 'a little part' of Hassan in Taliban-governed Afghanistan demonstrates great courage as well as a strong loyalty to those he holds dear.

While Baba is presented as the archetype of the bold, successful businessman, he is limited in his actions firstly by the attitudes of those around him, and secondly when he leaves his native culture and takes up residence in America. However, while Baba finds it difficult to adjust to life in a new culture, Amir demonstrates flexibility and resilience, and throughout *The Kite Runner* he develops the qualities of bravery, while continuing to display loyalty to Baba and, finally, Hassan. *The Kite Runner* demonstrates that success is not fixed and absolute, but can be measured and attributed to different people in different ways. It can be seen through Amir's realisation of his childhood dream of becoming a writer, and through his determination and success in rescuing Sohrab from a life of misery and abuse.

REFERENCES & READING

The text

Hosseini, Khaled, *The Kite Runner,* Bloomsbury, London, 2004.

Websites

Abbas, Zaffar, 'Pakistan's schisms spill into present', BBC World News, 7 October 2004, http://newswww.bbc.net.uk/1/hi/world/south_asia/3724082.stm

Afghanistan – Atlapedia Online, http://www.atlapedia.com/online/countries/afghan.htm

Afghanistan Country Study and Government Publications, Illinois Institute of Technology, http://www.atlapedia.com/online/countries/afghan.htm

Afghanistan, South Asian Free Media Association, http://www.gl.iit.edu/govdocs/afghanistan/

Guthmann, Edward, (untitled article), *San Francisco Chronicle*, 14 March 2005, http://www.sfgate.com/cgi-bin/article.cgi?f=/c/a/2005/03/14/DDGNDBOF471.DTL

Hansen, Liane, *Weekend Edition* – Sunday, National Public Radio, 27 July 2003, http://www.npr.org/templates/story/story.php?storyId=1358775

Miller, Kerri, 'Author is inspired by memories of Afghanistan', Minnesota Public Radio, 5 May 2004, http://news.minnesota.publicradio.org/programs/midmorning/listings/mm20040503.shtml

Hosseini, Khaled, Official website, http://www.khaledhosseini.com

Newspaper article

'Kite Runner author in East Bay', *The Providence Journal*, 6 May 2005, p.CO1.

Film

Kandahar, directed by Mohsen Makhmalbaf, distributed by Avatar Films, 2001.

Acknowledgement

Thanks to Abdul Zahir Shakoor for his kind help in checking the information on Afghanistan.